My friend lives
in an old house

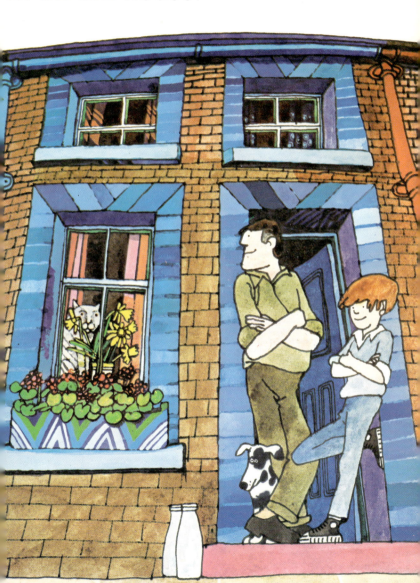

2

One day he had to move.

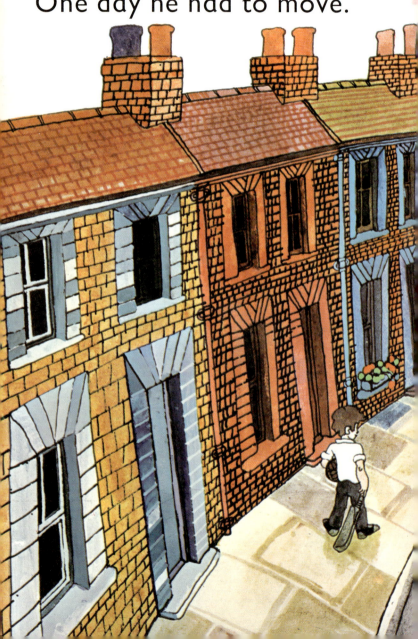

All the people had to move.
My friend went to live
in some new flats.

The old houses were all empty.
A gang of big boys broke the windows.

They climbed
into the old houses.
They played in
the old houses until one day
a big truck came.

The men had come
to pull down the houses.
Some of them climbed on
the roof.

They had big hammers.
They smashed the bricks.
The men broke the roof.

They pulled down chimneys.
They ripped off the tiles.

The other men took off
the doors and the windows.

10
Later on a bulldozer came.
The men put a rope through
one door and out of another.

They fixed the rope to the bulldozer. The bulldozer pulled and pulled and pulled.

The wall crashed down.
You couldn't see
the bulldozer for the dust.

Now you could see
the rooms inside the house.

You could see a bath.
You could see the stairs.
You could see the cooker.

14
My friend's house was gone.
Then the bulldozer pulled
down another one.

Two houses were gone.
Three houses were gone.
Four houses were gone.

16

One day all the houses
were gone.
The trucks went away.
The bulldozer went away
and we could play football.